THE EFE
PEOPLE OF THE ITURI RAIN FOREST

THE EFE

PEOPLE OF THE ITURI RAIN FOREST

by

ALEXANDRA SIY

DILLON PRESS
New York

Maxwell Macmillan Canada
Toronto

Maxwell Macmillan International
New York Oxford Singapore Sydney

ACKNOWLEDGMENTS

I want to thank Dr. Robert C. Bailey, co-director of the Ituri Project and associate professor of anthropology at UCLA, for his assistance. His knowledge and insights were invaluable for the completion of this book. Special thanks also to Dr. David Wilkie, who also co-directs the Ituri Project, for his suggestions and many wonderful photographs.

Many thanks also to the librarians at the Bethlehem Public Library in Delmar, New York. Finally, love and thanks to Eric Siy, my husband.

The following tales were adapted from *Among Congo Pigmies*, by Paul Schebesta, AMS Press, New York, New York, 1977: "The Elephant and the Lightning," "Heaven and Earth," "The Origin of Death," and the story told by the Lese villagers in chapter three. The story about being lost in the rain forest in chapter one was told to the author by Dr. Robert C. Bailey, who heard it from a group of Efe.

PHOTO CREDITS

Cover images courtesy of Dr. Robert C. Bailey
Dr. David Wilkie and Gilda Morelli: title page, 10, 15, 19, 21, 25, 26, 28, 34, 37, 42-43, 44, 47, 54, 58, 64; Dr. Robert C. Bailey: 30, 48, 53, 55.

Book design by Carol Matsuyama

LIBRARY OF CONGRESS CATALOGING-IN-PUBLICATION DATA

Siy, Alexandra.
    The Efe : people of the Ituri Forest / by Alexandra Siy. – 1st ed.
       p. cm. – (Global villages)
    Includes bibliographical references.
    Summary: Describes the culture and history of the Efe, a Pygmy tribe living in the rain forests of equatorial Africa, and explains how their environment and way of life are threatened by the encroachment of the industrial world.
    ISBN 0-87518-551-7
    1. Efe (African people)–Social life and customs–Juvenile literature. 2. Ituri Forest (Zaire)–Social life and customs–Juvenile literature. [1. Efe (African people) 2. Pygmies. 3. Ituri Forest (Zaire) 4. Rain forests–Zaire.] I. Title. II. Series.
DT650.E34S57   1993
967.51'004965–dc20   93-6717

Dillon Press
Macmillan Publishing Company
866 Third Avenue
New York, NY 10022

Maxwell Macmillan Canada, Inc.
1200 Eglinton Avenue East
Suite 200
Don Mills, Ontario M3C 3N1

Macmillan Publishing Company is part of the Maxwell Communication Group of Companies.

First edition

Printed in the United States of America
10 9 8 7 6 5 4 3 2 1

CONTENTS

Introduction
–6–

Fast Facts
–8–

CHAPTER 1 Forest Dwellers
–11–

CHAPTER 2 Tribal Wisdom
–22–

CHAPTER 3 The Lese Connection
–38–

CHAPTER 4 A Celebration of Life
–49–

CHAPTER 5 The Global Village
–56–

Activities
–65–

For Further Reading
–67–

Glossary
–68–

Index
–71–

INTRODUCTION

As the 1990s draw to a close, we look forward to not only a new century but a new millennium. What will the next thousand years bring for the planet earth and its people? And what aspects of our ancient past will we retain on our journey into a new time, a new world?

Today the world is already a vastly different place from what our great-grandparents would have imagined. People from distant parts of the planet can communicate within seconds. In less than 24 hours, you can fly around the world. Thanks to these and other remarkable advances in technology, the world has become a "global village."

In a sense, the peoples of the earth are no longer strangers, but neighbors. As we meet our "neighbors," we learn that now, more than ever before, our lives are intertwined. Indeed, our survival may depend on one another.

In one of the oldest rain forests in Africa, the Ituri Forest, an unusual group of people have made their home for hundreds of years. They call themselves the Efe, and they are among the last hunter-gatherers on earth. They are also the shortest people in the world. Commonly known as Pygmies, the Efe have managed to survive in their often-harsh jungle environment for centuries. Now, however, their future as a people is threatened.

Cash-producing coffee plantations have taken over large portions of the Efe homeland. Poor farmers from heavily populated areas of the African continent have also moved in, seeking free farmland. Although much of the Ituri Forest has been declared part of the Okapi Wildlife Reserve, the future of the Efe is uncertain because plans for the reserve do not address the rights of the Efe to their ancestral lands. As we learn more about these ancient forest-dwellers, we may find new ways to understand and respect all the peoples of the world.

FAST FACTS

CULTURE
The Efe live by hunting game in the Ituri rain forest; gathering honey, fruits, nuts, roots, plants, and certain insects; and trading with nearby villagers for vegetables, tobacco, metal tools, and cloth.

HUMAN HISTORY
The Efe have lived in the Ituri Forest for some 2,000 years. They are one tribe among several that are commonly called Pygmies.

NATURAL HISTORY
The Ituri Forest is relatively young compared to other rain forests around the world. However, it is one of the oldest rain forests in Africa.

GEOGRAPHY
The Ituri Forest is located on the equator in central Africa in the northeastern part of Zaire. The Efe live widely scattered in this region.

CLIMATE
The tropical climate is moist and warm with average rainfall about 65 inches a year and daytime temperatures averaging 85°F; there is a dry season from December to February.

GLOBAL IMPORTANCE
The Efe are one of the few remaining groups of people on earth who still live mostly by hunting and gathering. The Efe possess detailed knowledge of the plant and animal life native to African rain forests. The people have been studied by psychologists because their infants and children are cared for by numerous people besides their parents. The knowledge gained from these studies could be important to industrial societies that depend more and more on day-care centers. The Efe are also unique: They are the shortest people in the world.

CURRENT STATUS

The way of life of the Efe is threatened because their rain forest is in danger. New roads have brought large-scale plantation farming to the forest, which not only destroys parts of the forest but also disrupts the social and economic traditions of the native inhabitants. People from other parts of Africa are also migrating along the roads to the Ituri Forest in search of land to farm. Deforestation is a serious threat.

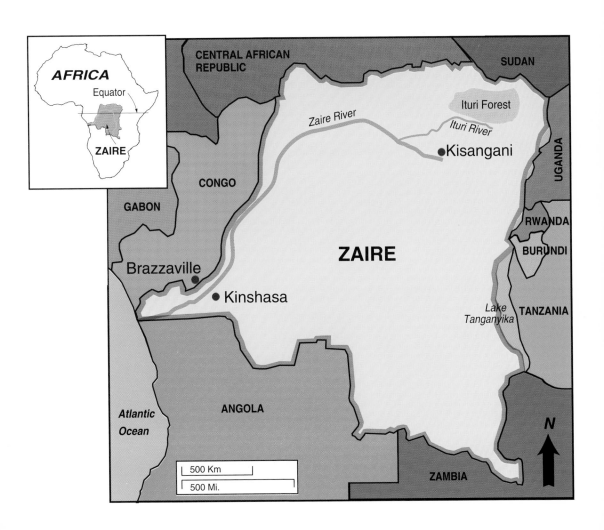

CHAPTER ONE

FOREST DWELLERS

In a **tropical** jungle in Africa, the people tell this story:

Once there was a man who liked to hunt alone. Sometimes he went hunting with his friends, but most of the time he went far into the forest by himself. He always knew where he was going and he never lost his way home. Sometimes he followed paths and sometimes he remembered his way by looking at the trees.

One day the man was hunting deep in the forest. He had just killed a monkey and was carrying it home on his back. Suddenly, he heard a voice in the trees.

"Chabo," said the voice.

When the man heard his name being called, he stopped to listen.

"Chabo," the voice called out again. And the man followed the voice.

Then the man saw some leaves ahead of him on the ground. The leaves made a path through the forest and the man followed it.

As he walked the man heard his name being called again, and again.

"Chabo, Chabo, Chabo..." said the voice. The man walked

Deep in the Ituri Forest, a lone Efe hunter takes aim at a tree-dwelling monkey.

faster and faster as he followed the trail of leaves. After a long while the man became very tired. He stopped and looked around. It was quiet and the trail of leaves had disappeared. The man was in a part of the forest he had never seen before.

Then the man knew he was lost. His body started shaking and he began to panic.

"I am lost!" he cried.

He looked all around but did not know which way to turn. In his terror he started to run. He ran and ran until he felt he couldn't run anymore. When he finally stopped it was almost dark. He looked up and saw ahead of him a tree that he had seen many times before.

"I am not lost!" he shouted. And he ran the rest of the way home. When he reached the camp the people met him.

"Chabo, you are shaking, you are frightened," they said.

And then the man told the people how the spirit Muri-Muri had called his name and made a path of leaves to nowhere, deep in the forest.

Very rarely, people who live in the African jungle get lost. Usually, they walk through the forest as easily and confidently as city dwellers find their way around city streets. The forest dweller, too, depends on landmarks–streams, hills, stumps, and very old trees–to help him find his way. But sometimes every tree looks unfamiliar.

It is difficult for people who have never visited or lived in the rain forest to imagine the emotions felt by someone who is lost there. Indeed, the rain forest has sparked the imagination for centuries. It is a place that has been both hated and loved by the few outsiders who have entered it and lived in it for a short time. It is from their accounts that the rest of the world has come to form images of the forest and of the people who make it their home.

THE ITURI FOREST

The African jungle is not the thick, vine-snarled jungle of Tarzan films. Instead, the rain-forest floor is rather open and bare. Towering into the sky are 300-year-old trees, blocking the sunshine. Shrubs, herbs, and a few young trees grow scattered on the forest floor, where sunlight is scarce.

Africa contains about 20 percent of the remaining tropical rain forests on earth. The Ituri Forest covers nearly 25,000 square miles, about the size of West Virginia. Most of the Ituri Forest lies in northeastern Zaire. The forest gets its name from the Ituri River, which flows through it.

Located on the equator, the Ituri Forest is warm (85°F) and humid (80 percent) year-round. But there are seasons. The dry season–when rains are infrequent–lasts about three months, from December to February. The rest of the year it rains and rains. The Ituri Forest receives about 65 inches of rainfall a year.

Like the tropical forests of South America and Asia, the

THE EFE

African rain forests are **biologically diverse**; they are rich in many species of plants and animals. Birds, bats, and monkeys live in the trees, feeding off fruits, flowers, and leaves. Unlike tropical rain forests on other continents, however, the jungles of central Africa have many animals that dwell on the ground as well as in the trees. Rodents, duikers (forest antelopes), elephants, buffalo, and okapis (forest giraffes) range over the forest floor searching for fallen fruits, nuts, and seeds. Most likely these animals moved into the Ituri Forest from the neighboring grasslands, or **savanna**, many thousands of years ago.

Of all the rain forests in Africa, the Ituri is home to the largest number of plant and animal species. It is also home to a unique group of people: the Efe (ef-FAY), who have lived there for perhaps 2,000 years.

THE EFE

Although the Efe live in the remote and isolated Ituri Forest, they are not a "lost" or unknown **tribe.** The Efe and their relatives have been studied by modern **anthropologists** and made legendary by ancient civilizations.

The Efe are one tribe in a large population of **indigenous**, or native, people commonly known as Pygmies. Each tribe follows its own traditions and speaks a different **dialect** than the others. In the Ituri Forest there are four Pygmy tribes: the Efe, the Sua, the Aka, and the Mbuti. Collectively, they are called the Bambuti.

The Ituri Forest. Hot and humid year-round, it is home to a great variety of plants and animals.

There are about six other tribes of Pygmies scattered across the rain forests of central Africa. Altogether, some 140,000 Pygmies live in Africa, making them the largest group of **hunter-gatherers** on earth. The Efe number about 5,500.

THE AFRICAN PYGMIES

African Pygmies. The words bring to mind images of an exotic tribe of miniature people who live in the dark jungles of deepest Africa. Indeed, for thousands of years the Pygmies have been legendary.

More than 4,000 years ago an Egyptian pharaoh sent out an army to look for the source of the Nile River. The expedition encountered a group of short people living in the rain forests of central Africa. The commander of the expedition sent a message to the pharaoh describing the people as "dancing dwarfs from the land of the spirits." The pharaoh ordered his general to return to Egypt with one of these "Dancers of God." There the story ends, with no one knowing whether a dancing forest person ever returned to Egypt.

But over the next 2,000 years Egyptian art and Greek literature were inspired by the people who became known as the Pygmies. In Greek the word *pygme* actually means the distance between a man's elbow and his knuckles. Over time this measurement–*pygme*–was used to describe the unusually small people of the African jungle.

A MYTHICAL PEOPLE

The ancient Greek poet Homer wrote in his famous *Iliad* about large birds called cranes that flew to Africa to battle with the Pygmies. In the Middle Ages, Arab traders brought home stories from Africa of dwarfs jumping out at them from beneath the ground and killing their comrades with poison arrows. These unbelievable tales convinced most of the world that the Pygmies were just a myth.

In 1699 an English doctor obtained some skeletons that were said to have been Pygmies. He decided that the Pygmies did not exist because his research concluded the skeletons were not human, but instead a kind of ape or monkey. Now scientists know the bones he studied were actually those of a chimpanzee.

During the 1800s the existence of the Pygmies was finally confirmed by several separate explorers who traveled into the African jungles. Although they recognized that the Pygmies were people, they also believed them to be "animal-like" human beings.

WESTERN SCIENTISTS

In 1870 the German **botanist** Georg Schweinfurth began his studies in the Ituri Forest. He observed that the Pygmies not only hunted and gathered foods for themselves, but also traded forest foods, such as wild meat and honey, with nearby villagers for garden crops and iron arrow tips. He concluded that the Pygmies had lived isolated in the forests for hundreds of years and that they had only recently begun to trade with outsiders.

The first anthropologist to study the Efe was Paul Schebesta. His work in the 1930s concluded that the Pygmies were unable to survive without trading for village foods. He believed that the Efe were almost entirely dependent on the neighboring villagers, a tribe known as the Lese (less-SAY).

The English anthropologist Colin Turnbull lived with a group of Pygmies for several years during the 1950s. His experiences led him to believe that the Pygmies only traded with the villagers for a "change of pace" from their forest life. He believed that they were not dependent on the villagers for their survival.

THE EFE

Since the 1970s several researchers have studied the Efe. Their work has shown that the Efe and Lese have a complex relationship. Many scientists now think that the relationship is **symbiotic**–meaning both groups of people need and benefit from each other.

But even today modern anthropologists still do not fully understand the Pygmies and their way of life. They wonder whether the Pygmies ever lived in the rain forests totally on their own–without villagers close-by.

Anthropologists are now looking for **archaeological** evidence, or the remains of an earlier culture, to help solve the mystery of these ancient people. But finding such evidence may be difficult. The warm and humid environment of the rain forest causes the remains of animals and plants to decay very quickly, leaving few **fossils** or other traces of former life behind. Another way to learn about the ancient past is to study the people who still live in the rain forests.

SHORT PEOPLE

One reason the Pygmies have interested scientists is that they are very short. Short people are defined as grown adult men who are less than 4'11". In tropical regions around the world, there are several groups of people who fit this description. These people are also known to some as Pygmies. There are short people in the Philippines, New Guinea, the Andaman Islands,

The Efe are the shortest people in the world. Adult women on average are only 4' 6" tall.

the Malay Peninsula, and South America. However, these distant groups are not related physically or culturally.

Today all Pygmies, whether in Africa or in other parts of the world, prefer to be called by their tribal names, the names they have given themselves. The word *Pygmy,* given to them by Western outsiders, is considered disrespectful.

The Efe are the shortest people in the world. Adult men average 4'8", adult women just 4'6"–the height of an average nine-year-old child in the United States.

Some scientists think that just living in a hot and humid environment favors a small size because small people do not overheat as quickly as large people. Therefore, these researchers conclude, small people had a better chance of surviving in hot and humid regions and shortness **evolved** as a characteristic.

Other scientists, however, believe food supply had more to do with the evolution of small size than climate did. Small people need less food to survive than large people. Small size would be a big advantage to people living in areas where food is in short supply. Although rain forests are rich in plant life, many tropical plants are poisonous, inedible, or difficult for humans to gather and prepare as food.

A LIVING LINK

Scientists now know that the Efe have developed, over many centuries, a unique way of life in the Ituri Forest. Today, however, their survival is threatened because the future of the forest itself is uncertain. Roads are being constructed throughout Africa, and the once-isolated rain forests are endangered. Coffee and oil-palm plantations are springing up along the roads, destroying large areas of forest. With the plantations come merchants and workers. Poor farmers from heavily populated areas of the continent also follow the new roads in search of free farmland. So many people place a great burden on the resources of the land. Wild **game**, for example, is becoming scarce, and rivers and other sources of water are becoming polluted.

If the forest and its indigenous inhabitants cannot survive, all the world will lose an irreplaceable **ecosystem**, a unique culture, and a living link to our ancient past. Perhaps even

An Efe child. The future of his tribe is at risk as outsiders take over large areas of his forest.

more important than being a link to our past, the Efe may represent a bridge to our future. Their way of life–their knowledge and wisdom–may not seem profound, or even relevant, to others. Yet the basic values that have ensured the Efe's survival in the Ituri Forest are important for everyone.

CHAPTER TWO

TRIBAL WISDOM

THE ELEPHANT AND THE LIGHTNING

One day the Efe were hunting elephant. They walked far from their camp and came upon a high mountain. They decided to follow the path leading up the mountain. At the top they came to the village of the Lightning. They looked all around and saw no one. So they squatted on the ground and waited in stillness.

At last the Lightning saw the strangers squatting in his village. He came down upon them with a terrific crash. But the hunters did not move. They continued to squat calmly on the ground.

"I'll teach you!" growled the Lightning, and darted down among them a second time. But the Efe didn't stir and the Lightning was astonished. Just then his daughter came up to him and said, "Look, father, those strangers have spears, just like those that hunters of elephants carry."

The Lightning asked the hunters why they had spears, and the Efe told him they were elephant hunters, too. The Lightning immediately became friendly and said, "An elephant has been trampling my garden for a long time. Please kill the elephant for me. I promise I will reward you if you do this for me."

The next morning the Efe looked for the elephant. As soon

as the elephant came in sight, an old hunter whispered to his son, "Go! Give him the first blow!"

The young man drew his sharpened spear. He ran under the elephant and thrust it through the belly. The huge elephant roared with pain and collapsed to the ground.

When the Lightning saw the dead elephant, he was very happy and prepared a celebration for the hunters. Everyone feasted on elephant meat until there was nothing left.

Then the Lightning brought the hunters safely down the mountain, where they found their own camp. And ever since, the Efe and the Lightning have been friends. The Efe are not afraid of him. He may flash and boom all around them, but he will not harm them.

For all the time the Efe have lived in the Ituri Forest, they never learned how to make a fire. Instead, they "possessed," or kept, the fire they found burning in trees that had been struck by lightning. All day and all night, year after year, fire was kept burning, because to find new fire was not an easy task.

The Efe never developed a written language, either. Yet the Efe are no less intelligent, rational, or curious than people who live in other societies. All their history and knowledge are preserved in an **oral tradition**. Stories and legends like "The Elephant and the Lightning" are told and retold around the campfire. Many of the tales provide detailed knowledge of the rain-forest ecosystem. And this great body of information is stored in the minds of the people, especially the **elders**. There is an African proverb that says: "When an elder dies it is like burning an entire library of books to the ground." The "library," however, is not truly lost when an elder dies, because he or she has already passed its wisdom and knowledge to the new generation.

BEING A CHILD

Efe children learn how to live in the rain forest in many ways. Their parents and other adults teach them skills. They also learn simply by watching others and through their own experience.

Boys learn to shoot with a bow and arrow and to make their own weapons before they are nine years old. They practice their aim by tossing fruit in the air and trying to hit it. These games, along with actual hunting trips, help young boys develop their shooting skills. They also learn much about the rain forest on these trips.

Girls go into the forest with their mothers on fishing and **foraging** trips. From these outings they learn which plants are edible and which are poisonous–this information alone could fill a **botany** book. But books will never be a part of a girl's education. She will never have a recipe book, a gardening book, a map of the forest, or a book about child care. Yet by the time she is a woman, she will know how to do everything to support and care for her family.

Many of the games children play involve activities that are

An Efe boy begins early in life to practice his hunting skills.

important for survival, such as target practice, tree climbing, and playing "dolls" with real babies. But Efe boys and girls, like children everywhere, play most games just for fun. Their toys are made from the materials found in the forest. A jump rope is easily made from a vine, and a playhouse is built out of the same materials used to build the family huts.

Like children everywhere, Efe kids love to play. The rain forest offers some special games, however, like making music with buzzing insects.

THE CAMP

The Efe live in family groups, known as **bands,** in small, temporary settlements, or camps. The basic social unit is the nuclear family. It consists of a father, mother, and their children. There may be several extended families in a camp. Extended families include brothers and their wives and children, unmarried sisters, and parents. Altogether, 10 to 30 people usually live in a camp.

Each nuclear family builds its own small (five feet wide and four feet high) dome-shaped hut out of bent saplings, leaves, and mud. The huts are constructed in a circle with the doors facing the center. This arrangement creates a common space used by all the people. Fires are kept in each hut as well as in the common space. The huts are used for sleeping, storing food, and for protection from the rain.

The Efe spend most of their time outside. People are rarely alone. A person's moods, as well as his or her daily habits, such as eating and bathing, are observed by all members of the band. This lack of privacy makes it important that people cooperate with one another. The Efe value getting along with others, sharing, and being tolerant.

The Efe have few belongings, and most are easily made from materials found in the forest. Sleeping mats are woven out of leaves, and stools are made by lashing together short sticks. Cooking equipment, such as pots and knives, are traded for with the Lese villagers. Some Efe wear clothes they have also

The Efe live in family groups in small, temporary settlements in the forest.

gotten through trade with the Lese.

The Efe are **seminomadic**–they move their homes through-out the forest several times during the year. From October to January and April through May, they live near the edge of the forest, within a 15-minute walk of a Lese village. During the other months, when hunting is best and honey is abundant, the Efe move deeper into the forest. However, they are never more than a day's walk from a village.

There is no one "in charge" of an Efe camp. The people do not have formal leaders or chiefs. Their society is an **egalitarian** one, which means it is based on the idea that everyone is treated equally. An elder, however, usually helps the group make decisions.

The respect given to an elder is not based on wealth or status, but instead on the knowledge and experience the person has accumulated over his or her lifetime. The Efe also recognize the abilities and talents of each individual. For example, a man who is exceptionally skilled at making hunting bows is honored for his talent. People are recognized for a wide range of abilities, including musical talent, hunting skills, and physical strength.

EFE "DAY CARE"

Efe women, who often work away from the camp, share child-care responsibilities with one another. From the time they are born, Efe children are cared for by many people besides their mothers. The children develop an attachment to everyone in the group, which is important for people who live in the difficult rain-forest environment. Survival in the jungle is only possible when people work closely together.

When a child is born, the infant is bathed and wrapped in cloth and then held by most of the women in the group before being cradled by his or her mother.

Young babies are rarely put down. Some scientists believe this behavior developed because Efe newborns are tiny and lose heat easily. Constant warmth through human contact could increase an infant's chances for survival. Babies nap in the arms

The Efe build dome-shaped huts from bent saplings, leaves, and mud.

of their mothers and other women instead of cradles or hammocks. When a mother is busy working, another woman or girl holds her child. Infants are returned to their own mothers for frequent feeding. At night mothers and babies sleep together.

Efe children benefit from this system of care because they **bond** with many people besides their mothers. They also receive quality care. Child abuse and neglect are unknown in Efe society.

HUNTERS AND GATHERERS: MEN AND WOMEN

Both women and men have specific roles in their community. In general, the women are the gatherers and the men the hunters.

A marriage of a woman and man brings together the skills needed for survival in the rain forest.

Efe usually marry when they are about 20 years old. In many parts of Africa a young man must "pay" for his bride. The bridal payment can be money, cattle, or other goods, or a promise to work for the bride's father for a year or more. But the Efe do not accumulate material wealth because they move around so much. Instead of "buying" his bride, an Efe man exchanges a woman from his band—usually his sister or cousin—for the woman he wants to marry. This arrangement is called "sister exchange" because his sister will marry one of the men from his bride's band.

There is no marriage ceremony in Efe society. A young man may present his bride's father with an antelope as a gift and as a request for his blessings. Two people are considered married when they begin living together in their own hut. However, the marriage is not looked upon as permanent until the couple has a child. If they do not have a child within a year or two, the marriage may end in "divorce" and the man and woman may find new marriage partners.

Efe women do most of the work at the camp to keep it running smoothly. They gather firewood, fetch water, and cook. However, Efe men also cook and take care of the children when their wives are away from the camp gathering food or trading.

THE ARCHERS

Known as the "archers of the rain forest," the Efe kill most of their game with bows and arrows. They use spears to hunt some large animals, such as wild pigs, forest buffalo, and elephants. Although it is illegal to kill elephants in Zaire, the Efe hunt them anyway, using metal-tipped spears. An elephant kill is a rare event, occurring once every four or five years.

The Efe hunt and eat more than 45 different kinds of animals. The most common are antelope, or duikers, which make up 90 percent of the game taken by the people.

A hunt begins early in the morning. The men gather around a fire, smoke tobacco in clay pipes, and prepare their tools. They straighten and harden the shafts of their arrows over the fire. They tighten their bowstrings and make sure their metal arrow tips are secured tightly. They fasten guards made of monkey skin to their wrists to protect themselves from the stinging snap of the bow.

The Efe believe certain leaves possess magical qualities and they add these to the fire. The hunters hold their bows and arrows in the smoke–it is hoped this will improve their hunting success. Some of the leaves are also rubbed on the bowstrings. Their hunting dogs are also passed through the smoke.

Hunting dogs are the only domestic animals kept by the Efe. They belong to a certain breed, known as basenji, which whines but rarely barks.

The Efe perform a certain **ritual**, known as a *mota*, which they believe will ensure a successful hunt. The *mota* is led by one man, an experienced hunter called the *aetasi*. He signals when it is time for the group to begin the hunt. Several archers walk ahead for a mile or more and arrange themselves in a large semicircle, where they stand very still with their bows flexed, ready to shoot.

Two or three men follow with hunting dogs that wear wooden bells around their necks. These men and the dogs run through the forest making as much noise as possible. The clanging bells and shouting hunters serve to drive game out of hiding and toward the waiting archers.

The archers let their arrows fly when an animal appears. Often the animal is only wounded and must be tracked down by the dogs. The archers conduct several *mota* until they are satisfied with their catch. When an animal is killed, the Efe usually butcher it immediately. Each hunter gets a share of the meat, but the first man to hit the animal gets the largest and most prized share: the hindquarters and the liver. The owner of the dogs gets the head and a front quarter. The game is wrapped in tilipi leaves to be carried back to the camp. Believing that nothing should be wasted, the Efe eat every part of the animal, even the marrow inside the bones.

If the archers are unsuccessful at hunting, they will return to camp with food they have gathered, such as mushrooms,

A hunter and his son with all the tools of their trade, including a special hunting dog equipped with a wooden bell.

fallen fruits, tortoises, or birds' eggs.

Efe archers also spend a lot of time hunting alone. They kill monkeys with poison-tipped arrows. They hide in fruit trees and shoot duikers when the animals come to feed.

THE HONEY HUNT

Men also "hunt" for honey. Sometimes a man will go out alone to look for honey-filled beehives, but usually the Efe go in small groups of two to five men. A hunter blows on a honey flute, a harsh-sounding whistle, when he finds a hive. The men mark the trees containing hives and return later to harvest the honey.

Summer is the best time of the year for collecting honey, and the Efe look forward to it with excitement. During the summer months–June to September–bees gather nectar from the large flowering *rofo* trees.

Honey is a delicious and nutritious forest food. But it is also difficult and dangerous to obtain. Beehives are usually found high in the rain-forest **canopy**. Often a hunter must climb a smaller tree first and then transfer to the taller tree in which the nest is located. Sometimes he will face a flurry of stinging bees defending their hive.

As a honey harvest begins, the men quickly weave baskets from leaves and make a strong cord by twisting vines together. One basket is filled with smoldering coals and leaves that make a thick smoke. Another basket holds an ax that will be used to slash open the hive.

The hunter who will harvest the honey climbs to a branch above the hive. He uses the vine cord to help him swing from branch to branch. The baskets are hoisted up with cord by two men who have climbed onto the lower branches. One man holds the smoldering basket below the hive so that the smoke swirls into the nest, causing the bees to become temporarily inactive.

The other man passes the basket holding the ax to the hunter above the nest. The basket also contains a body sling made from vines. The hunter slips into the sling and fastens it to a branch. Then he lowers himself, upside down, until he comes face-to-face with the hive. Quickly, he cuts a hole in the hive and plunges his hand inside. He grabs chunks of honeycomb and puts them in the basket.

Sometimes the hunter throws pieces of honeycomb to the anxious men waiting on the ground. These pieces often contain more beeswax, larvae, and pollen than honey, but the men eagerly eat it all.

The hunters eat as much honey as their stomachs will hold. Sometimes there is nothing left for the women and children at the camp. But usually, there is enough honey for the rest of the camp, and for the Lese villagers as well. Over the course of a year, honey provides the Efe with about 14 percent of their food.

FRUITS AND FISH

Although not as prized as honey, a variety of other foods are harvested from the forest. Certain fruits, nuts, insects, mush-rooms, and **tubers** are collected by Efe women. They usually eat some of them on the spot and then carry the rest back to camp.

Iswa, or termites, are a good source of protein. Roasted and pounded into a nutritious paste, *iswa* are often wrapped in a convenient leaf package and carried and eaten on the trail. The olivelike fruits of the canary tree are a preferred forest food, especially when eaten with honey.

Although a lot of different kinds of plants grow in the rain forest, many are not edible. And those that are good to eat may grow far apart in the forest. Sometimes a person may have to

Going fishing: The Efe sometimes step into the water and catch fish with their hands.

search for hours to find two trees bearing the same kind of fruit.

When plants are found and carried home, women often spend a lot of time preparing them for eating. For example, certain forest yams must be peeled, sliced, and soaked in a mixture of water and ashes for at least a day before they can be boiled and eaten, and they are never as tasty as yams cultivated in the Lese gardens.

Women also fish in small streams throughout the forest. They usually use poles and nets. Sometimes they dam a stream and catch the fish with their hands. On the stream bank they cook some for themselves and carry the rest back to camp for their families.

Altogether, the food gathered and hunted by the Efe accounts for just one-third of the food they eat. The rest of their diet comes from trading with the Lese villagers.

CHAPTER THREE

THE LESE CONNECTION

The Lese villagers tell this story:

Long ago a Lese man built his house among the rocks near the edge of the forest. Around his house he would dance, and his magic dances did great harm to the Efe who lived nearby.

One day the old woman who lived with the man noticed an Efe hunter walking near her garden. She lured the hunter into a trap. "A wild beast is destroying our garden," she said. "I beg you to kill it. Grunt like a pig, and it will appear at once. Then you can kill it."

The hunter did as the woman had told him. He grunted and waited for the boar to appear. But the boar did not come. Instead, the grunting brought the Lese out of his house. The man started to dance his magic dance and jangle his bells.

The hunter aimed at the man, but his bowstring snapped, because the old woman had previously cut it half through. The man then killed the hunter and all the other Efe hunters who were waiting in the field. The only Efe to escape was the elder. The old woman went into the field and gathered the bodies and brought them home and ate them.

The elder was now the only survivor of all the Efe hunters. Later on, the old woman tried to trick him, too. She told him to go into the garden to kill the wild pig that was doing such terrible damage to the banana trees. When he reached the garden, he saw the great damage that had been done, but he also saw that the whole field was covered with blood.

He sent the old woman home and tested his bowstring. The string snapped, and he immediately suspected the woman was trying to trick him. He took a spare string, which he always carried, and fixed it to his bow. Then he started to grunt, and the Lese man appeared and started to dance.

The elder aimed and shot an arrow into the man's chest. The man ran and staggered until he collapsed, dead, among the rocks. The elder cut off the man's arm and fled into the forest.

In the forest the elder met all the Efe women, who were waiting for him. Together they traveled until they came to a great river and waded through it, to the other side.

In this legend the Lese couple tried to trick the Efe and devour all of them. Thanks to the cleverness and skill of the elder, the band of Efe was not entirely wiped out. Although the remaining people retreated safely into the forest, the legend doesn't end by saying they lived there, alone, happily ever after. The curious decision made by the elder to cut off the Lese's arm and carry it into the forest may symbolize the bond that exists between the Efe and Lese.

The Efe have lived in close association with Lese villagers for at least 400 years. The Efe also have legends that describe their relationship with the Lese, and both groups of people tell stories about the origins of each other from their own points of view.

For years anthropologists have debated the extent and significance of the Efe's attachment to the Lese. Today scientists understand that the Efe are not only hunter-gathers of the forest. They are also forest merchants–trading meat, honey, wild fruits, building materials, and labor for garden crops, tobacco, cooking pots, metal arrow tips, knives, and cloth.

ANCIENT GARDENS

Farming in the African rain forests started about 2,000 years ago when Arab traders brought tropical Asian crops, such as bananas, to Africa. Before Asian crops were introduced, farming wasn't possible in the African rain forests. Native African crops, such as millet and **sorghum**, could not survive in the hot and humid environment.

Many years later, during the 1500s, Portuguese slave traders brought several kinds of food to Africa that were originally grown by native South Americans. Manioc (also known as cassava), corn, peanuts, beans, squash, and sweet potatoes gradually began to be cultivated in rain-forest gardens.

The Lese were among the first farmers in the Ituri Forest. They had been farmers in the bordering savanna, which is now part of the nation of Sudan. When they obtained the new tropical crops, they moved deep into the rain forest.

FARMING IN THE FOREST

Today the Lese live and farm very much like their ancestors did 400 years ago. They live in small villages of 15 to 100 people. They used to move and set up new villages every five to ten years. They could not stay in one spot for too long because rain-forest soil is poor. Gardens are productive for just one or two years. Old gardens must be left **fallow**, or unplanted, for about 20 years before they can be planted again.

Now villages are more permanent. The Lese remain in them for about 15 years. This change is a result of a road built by Belgian colonists in the 1930s. The road gives the farmers greater access to the forest, where they can plant several garden plots without moving the entire village.

Each village house cuts down about one acre of land every year. The Lese men carefully choose a place for a garden. The garden must be within walking distance of the houses because the women will have to go there every day. The men also look for places that were farmed by their relatives 20 years earlier. These patches of forest are still young and the trees are easier to cut down than those in older areas.

Like their ancestors, the Lese practice **slash-and-burn agriculture.** In December the garden site is prepared by the

A quiet moment in a Lese village as an evening storm approaches

men. They use axes to chop down the trees. Usually, the axes are quite dull–many are made from truck suspension springs found along the road. Often Efe men help the Lese clear the site.

After about a week the garden site is a mess of fallen trees and branches. Now the women and girls weave through the tangle, poking manioc and banana stalks into the ground. For the rest of the dry season, the garden is left untouched. The leaves and branches are dried by the sun and provide enough cover to protect the underlying soil from the scorching rays.

In February the garden is set on fire. The dead trees don't

burn completely and the fire is not hot enough to dry out the soil. But an important fertilizer is produced in the ashes of burnt wood. This fertilizer helps the newly sprouted manioc and banana plants grow and puts important **nutrients** in the soil for other crops that will soon be planted. Planting the garden is done by all the people. The men poke holes in the ground with a stick, and the women and girls, both Lese and Efe, drop in peanut, squash, and corn seeds. The garden grows and is harvested at intervals for the next 15 months. Both the soil and the crops are protected from the burning sun and heavy rains by the patchwork nature of the garden.

Slash-and-burn agriculture is successful in the rain forest because the gardens are kept small and moved frequently. The Lese are keenly aware of the seasonal changes in the forest and plan their slashing, burning, planting, and harvesting around the wet and dry seasons.

Slash-and-burn agriculture gives the fragile forest ecosystem a chance to regenerate, or grow back. When a garden patch is no longer cultivated, it provides **habitat** for plants that require a lot of sunlight. This is the first stage of **succession** that occurs in a healthy forest ecosystem.

WOMEN'S WORK

Once the garden is planted, the Lese men have finished most of their work for the year. They may weave a few baskets, make

An Efe girl helps her mother tend a Lese garden.

some tools, or build a hut, but most of their time is spent socializing with one another.

But Lese women have just begun the demanding work that never seems to end. Every day they toil in the gardens–weeding and harvesting. In the village they also care for the children, cook the meals, carry firewood and water, and wash clothes. Lucky for them, they have some help.

Efe women assist the Lese women with their seemingly impossible work schedule. They gather firewood, carry water, and collect wood for building huts. They help plant the fields and work in the gardens. In exchange for *shamba,* or garden labor, the Efe receive vegetables. Two-thirds of the food eaten by the Efe–mostly manioc roots and leaves, peanuts, bananas, and sweet potatoes–is grown in Lese gardens.

CLOSE TIES

Although the Efe and Lese have close ties, there is tension between the two groups. The Lese are prejudiced against the Efe and consider them socially inferior. For example, Lese woman do not marry Efe men because they think they are "beneath" them. Also, because the Efe are so skilled at living in the forest, the Lese consider them more "animal-like" than other people. An Efe often calls his trading partner "my *muto,*" or "my villager," and a Lese refers to his partner as "my Efe." However, in the case of the Lese, his expression often implies

Lese men use leaves to "tile" the roof of a hut in their village.

that he "owns" the Efe.

Often an Efe **clan** will be associated with a Lese village for several generations, making these ties of "ownership" seem real. For example, children and grandchildren of Efe and Lese elders continue to trade with one another as their parents and grandparents did before them.

But the Lese like to think they have more control over the Efe than they really do. Sometimes these long associations are broken when the Efe move to a different part of the forest to take advantage of better hunting or to escape food shortages caused by a regional drought. Upon moving, the Efe quickly associate themselves with other Lese villages.

A CELEBRATION OF LIFE

HEAVEN AND EARTH

Long ago, at the beginning, the earth was up there where heaven is now, and heaven was down here. But the Efe were hungry because all the food was on the earth, and there was nothing to eat in heaven.

So the Efe asked their Creator, Toré, if he would help them. Toré agreed, and the earth with all its food supplies fell down below, to the position it is in now. And then heaven went up in its place.

When an Efe dies, part of his spirit, or *megbe,* goes up there to heaven. Another part of the *megbe* enters his totem. And the rest of the *megbe* becomes a spirit called Lodi who lives in the forest with the rest of the Lodi spirits.

–This is what the elders say.

The earth provides the Efe with everything they need for survival. But the Efe do much more than just survive in the rain forest. Their way of life, or **culture**, is filled with ceremonies, music, and dance.

Every clan has a **totem**, a symbol of an animal by which the group is known. The Efe believe that the totem animal gave birth

All dressed up for an ima celebration

to the first ancestor of the clan, and they consider it holy.

Leopards and chimpanzees are common totems among the Efe. Clans that share the same totem believe that they came from a common ancestor. Clan members are often known by the name of their totem.

The totem animal is always **taboo**. For example, if the totem is a chimpanzee, clan members may not touch, kill, or eat any chimpanzees. The Efe believe that if a clan member has contact with a chimpanzee, he or she will become ill or die.

Such beliefs are considered superstitious by outsiders. But every culture has its own beliefs that often serve to help the people survive. While the Efe's beliefs may seem strange to outsiders, the beliefs of outsiders often seem meaningless to the Efe. In their forest world, the Efe have come to explain the meaning of life, and they celebrate it–every day.

RITES OF PASSAGE

Celebrations do not follow a formal time pattern. In fact, the Efe do not keep track of time. No one, for example, knows exactly how old he or she is. No birthdays are ever celebrated. However, like many **traditional** societies, the Efe and Lese mark the transition from childhood to maturity with certain rituals. We call these **initiation ceremonies** or **rites of passage**.

A girl's passage into womanhood is celebrated with a special ceremony known as the *ima*. The *ima* was traditionally a Lese ceremony that is now also a part of Efe culture. The participation of the Efe in an *ima* is crucial because they provide music for the celebration. They also make special medicines and dyes from rain-forest plants that are use in the *ima*.

When a girl begins to **menstruate**, she is ready to go into the *ima* hut that has been built in the Lese village. There she will stay for a least a month, often with one or more other Efe or Lese girls. During this time the women elders instruct the girls, answering questions about sexuality and offering other important information they will need as adults. The girls also learn special songs and dances that will be part of the *ima* celebration.

The girls, however, are not totally secluded in the hut. Sometimes young men push their way through a barrier of women and enter the hut. A girl may choose to have a sexual relationship with one of the men. Often a girl chooses her future husband from the group of men who have spent time in the *ima* hut. Occasionally, an Efe woman will marry a Lese man, but Lese women never marry Efe men.

All girls participating in the *ima* must wear a special bark cloth around their waists. The bark can be obtained from many kinds of trees, but some Efe think fig trees are best for cloth making. The bark is stripped from the tree with a knife and pounded flat with an old elephant tusk. Then it is washed and left to dry in the sun. The women paint the material, transforming it into elaborately decorated pieces of artwork.

The women use dyes prepared from charcoal, fruits, herbs, and *ndo,* a kind of wood. A "pen" made from a thin sliver of palm wood is used to paint the designs. It takes a least one day to decorate the cloth. During this time the rest of the people in the camp use the red, black, and yellow dyes to paint designs on one another's bodies. Lese and Efe women also weave cord made from palm leaves into bands and belts.

The night before the *ima* celebration begins, the women elders and the girls in the *ima* hut practice certain traditional dance steps and songs. The rest of the village is alive with the sounds of drums, singing, and clapping. Many people gather in a large meeting hut, built especially for the celebration.

Just before daybreak the girls are washed and dressed in their new bark cloths, bands, and belts. Their bodies are painted with dyes and smeared with white clay. As the sun rises the *ima* begins. The young women are carried outside on chairs. High above the crowd, they lead the procession to the center of the village. The people eat, drink, dance, sing, and lavish their attention on the young women. The festival lasts for three days, ending when the food and drink and energy of the dancers run out.

THE TORÉ

While the *ima* celebrates a girl's passage to womanhood, another ceremony honors certain elders as they approach death. It is

Painting the bark cloth the girls will use in the ima celebration

known as the Toré, and it is a secret ceremony. Only men and women who are members of the Toré secret society may participate.

Efe and Lese usually gather for the Toré to honor an elder while he or she is still alive. Sometimes a Toré is held for a respected elder who has died. The ceremony is held in a special place outdoors in a Lese village, and it lasts for about a month.

During the Toré men play seven-foot-long instruments made from the bark of fig trees. The sounds they make are like

Efe women decorate children as they prepare to attend ima *festivities.*

During the Toré ceremony, Efe and Lese men play seven-foot-long instruments that sound like the trumpeting of elephants.

the low-pitched trumpeting of elephants. At the same time, men and women dance in a circle and sing special Toré songs.

SONGS TO THE WIND

The Efe also have songs and dances for every day. Often the people sing as they work together. For example, while cooking lunch the women may break into song. Their music seems to have a magical effect–touching the inner spirits of the people and reaching out to the deep and dark forest all around.

CHAPTER FIVE

THE GLOBAL VILLAGE

THE ORIGIN OF DEATH

In the beginning, people did not die at all. In those days, Muri-Muri, a forest spirit, gave a pot to a toad. Inside the pot was something called death. The spirit ordered the toad to be careful not to break the pot, because if he did, death would escape. If death got out, the spirit warned, all people would be doomed to die.

The toad went on his way and met a frog who offered to carry the pot for him. The toad hesitated at first. But the pot was very heavy, so he eventually handed the pot to the frog and warned him to be very careful with it. The frog hopped away with the pot.

The pot slipped from the frog's grip and smashed on the ground. Death escaped from the pot and for the first time entered the forest. And that is how people came to die.

We can only guess why the Efe came to tell this short story about death. Why would the forest spirit entrust something as powerful and mysterious as death to a foolish toad? And why would the toad trust the clumsy frog with the fragile pot?

Perhaps it is easier to place the blame for such a blunder on a small, often disliked creature such as a frog. Or perhaps it wouldn't matter who was given the pot, because sooner or later it would break–making death inevitable.

LIVING WITH DEATH

Every person will die someday, and every culture has its own ways of dealing with death. But death doesn't visit all societies equally. In the Ituri Forest the Efe face death every day. It is difficult to survive in the hot and humid rain forest. For example, 22 percent of Efe children die before they are 5 years old. Because so many infants and children die, the average life expectancy of the Efe is just 38 years. Some Efe, though, do manage to survive until they are 75 or 80 years old.

Most deaths result from diseases such as pneumonia, **malaria**, **dysentery**, and **leprosy**. Many diseases are caused by **parasites**, organisms that live on or in the human body. The Efe make their own medicines from forest plants, but these are not as effective as modern medicines. Some outsiders believe that the Efe ought to receive modern medical care. And the Efe themselves would gladly accept help if it were available to them.

In the past the Efe had no hope of eliminating the deadly diseases, because they lived nearly isolated from the rest of the world. Today, however, their forest is not the remote, rarely visited place of long ago. More and more, the outside world is influencing the people who live in the Ituri Forest.

It's not easy to survive in the tropical rain forest. While the Efe prepare many medicines from plants, the people could be helped a lot by modern drugs.

A WIDER VILLAGE: THE WORLD

Like people everywhere, the Efe are part of a larger community – the **global village**. The global village is our planet earth and all the diverse peoples who live here. All people have common needs: clean water and air, food, and shelter. Yet they have different ways of acquiring them. People also have different spiritual beliefs, customs, and ideas about life.

In the past nations have been able to live pretty much apart from one another. The world seemed like a big place, with endless frontiers. But now it is clear that the earth isn't so big after all.

Today people thousands of miles apart can communicate

within seconds. They can travel to once-remote places and even bring back videos that document their experience. The ability to communicate so swiftly with others is changing how people think about one another. Places like Somalia, once strange and remote to Americans, have become familiar sights on television screens. In 1992 the faces of famine-stricken children moved thousands of American troops halfway across the globe.

THE RIPPLE EFFECT

Although there are nearly six billion people on the earth, every individual has an impact on the world in some way. Like a pebble thrown in a pond, the action of just one person can ripple outward, touching the lives of many others.

Not every action, of course, has a good effect on others. People living in industrial societies want natural resources, such as oil and timber, that are often obtained from poorer countries–referred to as the **Third World**. The ripple effect in this case can damage the environment and hurt local native communities.

But native people such as the Efe are beginning to be noticed and heard by the rest of the world. Their "voices" are creating a ripple that is touching the lives of distant people living in vastly different cultures. Their message to the world stresses the rights of indigenous people to choose their own futures and control the destiny of the lands they have lived on for generations.

CHOICES AND CHANGE

Over the centuries the Efe made choices that affected how they live in their environment. Their way of life has changed slowly over long periods of time, allowing the people and their environment time to adjust to new ways.

For example, as the Efe traded more and more with the Lese, they eventually lost their own language. Over time the Efe adopted the language of the Lese. The change from one language to another was slow enough so that ancient legends and important information were not lost. Even today some forest plants have names that were originally part of the ancient Efe language.

If given the choice, the Efe would accept some changes, such as health care and education, that would benefit their lives. But other changes, such as those the government of Zaire wants to impose, may not be welcomed.

EXPLOITING THE FOREST

The economy of Zaire is weak, and officials in the government are eyeing the rain forests as a way to make money. Huge areas in the Zaire River basin have been cleared. The forests are cut for paper pulp, lumber, and charcoal. So far the Ituri Forest has not been logged because the land is very hilly and the roads are poor, making it too expensive to move the lumber to the Atlantic coast for export.

Large-scale agriculture is another way the government hopes to strengthen the economy. Cash crops, such as coffee and oil palm, are grown on large plantations. These have had the greatest impact on the Ituri Forest. Often laborers from outside the forest are hired to work on them. These people bring their families and set up permanent villages nearby, where they plant crops for their own use. After a few years the soil near the village is depleted and the farmers need to clear more land. After several years large areas of rain forest are destroyed.

Deforestation presents a serious threat to the fragile rain-forest ecosystem. The tall trees hold the soil in place. Once they are gone and the soil is washed away, the forest cannot grow back. Instead, grasses may grow in its place. This is how a rain forest can someday become a grassland, or even a desert.

LOCAL CHANGE AND THE EFE

In some parts of the Ituri Forest, plantations are changing the way the Efe have "done business." When a plantation is set up, it attracts many workers. The result is a local population boom. Although the workers can grow their own manioc and other vegetables, they cannot raise animals for meat. (Rain-forest tsetse flies present a continual threat of cattle disease.) This creates a big demand for wild game, which in turn has brought about a new class of merchants from outside: meat traders.

At first glance it would seem that the high demand for meat would benefit the Efe, who are skilled at hunting. The meat traders travel into the forest to trade with them, exchanging food, tobacco, and other items for game. The traders bring the meat to the Lese villages and sell it to the people. As a result, the Efe no longer have to travel into the villages to trade.

These Efe have gained a measure of independence from the Lese villagers, but at a high price: They have lost the security that was part of the partnership. The relationship with the traders is not permanent; when game becomes scarce in one part of the forest, the traders move on to other areas. In order to survive, these Efe then need to reestablish ties with a Lese village. The resulting partnership, however, is often strained, because the Lese feel they can no longer rely on the Efe.

The breakdown of the traditional bonds between the Efe and the Lese is forcing some Efe to abandon their hunting-gathering way of life. These Efe must settle in villages and compete with outsiders for land and jobs. In the village world the Efe are on the lowest rung of the social ladder. They are discriminated against and are forced to take the worst-paying jobs and the least productive land. These Efe have lost their independence and their cultural heritage.

PLANTATIONS AND LESE FARMERS

Just as some Efe have become dependent on the meat traders, some Lese have become dependent on the plantations. Lese villages close to plantations are switching to a **market economy**. In the market economy Lese villagers earn wages by working

Lese villagers shop at a market set up once a week near the plantation where they work.

on the plantations and use the money to buy meat from the meat traders instead of trading with the Efe. They also spend some of their money on products available at the plantation store.

But in order to earn enough to buy meat and other goods, the Lese must spend most of their time working on the plantation. As a result, they plant small gardens that produce just enough to feed their own families. If an emergency arises, such as an illness or a death in the family, these Lese cannot work on the plantation *or* care for the family garden.

In the past the Efe provided meat and labor to help the Lese through such emergencies. In return they knew they could count on the Lese in times of need. This relationship provided a kind of

security that no longer exists in the new market economy. Often Lese plantation workers fall into debt and must work long hours to pay what they owe. Despite their hard work many families lack adequate protein in their diets and cannot afford to buy important goods. In this way the plantation system creates poverty in a community that once produced enough for all its people.

CHILDREN OF THE FOREST

The Efe think of themselves as "children" of the forest. They do not consider themselves superior to the forest, but believe that they belong to it. They know they cannot survive as a people without it. In the past some outsiders sought to study the Efe because their way of life was so different from that of most of the earth's people. Often the Efe were idealized for the seemingly "simple" life they led in an unspoiled tropical "paradise." Just as often they were derided as "primitive savages."

Today we can appreciate the Efe for who they are–fellow citizens of planet earth. In Efe society material wealth is not important. The bonds between people are what really matter. Are the Efe "better" people than the rest of us? Not really. The Efe are what they are because they *have* to be. Centuries of survival in the rain forest would not have been possible without the values of cooperation and sharing. Perhaps all people in our global village can learn from the values cherished by the people of the Ituri Forest.

ACTIVITIES

1. Help the Efe and Lese help themselves by supporting the Ituri Fund.
The Ituri Fund was created by a group of concerned anthropologists,
doctors, and scientists who have been working in the Ituri Forest since
the early 1980s. For information on how you can help, write to:

Ituri Fund	or	Ituri Fund
Cultural Survival		Dr. Robert C. Bailey
c/o Ted MacDonald		Department of Anthropology
215 First Street		UCLA
Cambridge, MA 02142		Los Angeles, CA 90024

2. Write a letter on behalf of the Efe and Lese. Most of the Ituri Forest
has been declared part of the Okapi Wildlife Reserve, which is similar
to a national park. So far the Efe and Lese have not be consulted in the
process of making plans for the reserve. By writing to the World Wide
Fund for Nature, you can influence this decision-making process. Keep
your letter short and make these points:

- The Efe and Lese should have a say in the plans for the Okapi
  Wildlife Reserve, because they depend on the resources of the
  forest.
- The Efe and the Lese should have the right to continue to live in
  their traditional ways if they so choose.

Send your letter to:

Director of Africa and Madagascar
World Wide Fund for Nature, International
Avenue du Mont Blanc
1196 Gland
Switzerland

3. Create a storytelling tradition in your own family. Ask your parents
or grandparents to tell you stories they liked hearing as children, or
ask them to tell you about the things they did as children. If your

grandparents live far away, send them a blank audio cassette and ask them to record their stories on tape.

4. Learn how to get involved in issues concerning indigenous people. There are several organizations and publications available to concerned young people:

Crayon Power is an environmental action magazine for kids. Every issue is filled with pictures you can color, cut out, fold, and send to the adults who make important decisions affecting the earth. For more information, write to *Crayon Power*, P.O. Box 34, Jersey City, NJ 07303.

Cultural Survival is a nonprofit organization that is working on behalf of indigenous peoples around the world. It is involved in projects that buy rain-forest products (such as Brazil nuts) that have been harvested by indigenous peoples. The products are sold to companies that use them in cookies, candies, and other products. These products are available to schools and other organizations for fund-raising projects. For more information write: Cultural Survival, 215 First Street, Cambridge, MA 02142.

Skipping Stones is a magazine about traditions and cultures around the world. Children from around the world are invited to contribute artwork, photos, and writings. For information call 503-342-4956 or write: *Skipping Stones,* P.O. Box 3939, Eugene, OR 97403-0939.

Young Survival is a special membership category for kids in the organization Survival International. If you join, you will receive an "action pack" that explains how you can get involved in the issues that affect indigenous people. For more information write: Survival International, 310 Edgware Road, London, United Kingdom, W2 1DY.

In your letters to the above groups ask them if they plan to feature the Efe in any of their publications. Include reasons why you think the Efe would be an important tribe for people to learn about.

FOR FURTHER READING
(AND LISTENING)

Bailey, Robert C. "The Efe: Archers of the African Rain Forest." *National Geographic,* November 1989.

Bebey, Francis. *African Music: A People's Art.* Chicago: L. Hill Books. 1975.

Bleeker, Sonia. *The Pygmies: Africans of the Congo Forest.* New York: Morrow Junior Books. 1968.

Burger, Julian. *The Gaia Atlas of First Peoples.* New York: Anchor Books/ Doubleday. 1990.

Collins, Mark (ed.). *The Last Rainforests: A World Conservation Atlas.* New York: Oxford University Press. 1990.

Duffy, Kevin. *Children of the Forest.* New York: Dodd, Mead. 1984.

Kraft, Marty, John Mcleod and Chris Wells. *Earth Day In Your School and Community.* Kansas City: Heartland All Species Project. 1993.

Maybury-Lewis, David. *Millenium: Tribal Wisdom and the Modern World.* New York: Viking. 1992.

Musgrove, Margaret. *Ashanti to Zulu: African Traditions.* New York: Dial Books for Young Readers. 1976.

"Polyphony of Deep Rain-Forest/The Music of Pygmy in Ituri" (Ethnic Sound Series 4/JVC/VID-25015) This recording features "sanza" or thumb-piano rhythms and traditional call-and-response singing. The songs are about elephants, bees, crickets, and other creatures of the Ituri Forest. It is available on compact disc.

Ranger Rick's Nature Scope/Rain Forests: Tropical Treasures. Washington, D.C.: National Wildlife Federation. 1989.

Reynolds, Jan. *Sahara: Vanishing Cultures Series.* San Diego: Harcourt Brace Jovanovich. 1992.

Turnbull, Colin. *The Peoples of Africa.* New York: The World Publishing Co. 1962.

_____*The Forest People.* New York: Simon and Schuster. 1961.

Wilkie, D. S., and G. A. Morelli. "Coming of Age in the Ituri." *Natural History.* October 1991.

_____"Pitfalls of the Pygmy Hunt." *Natural History.* December 1988.

GLOSSARY

anthropologist–a person who studies people, including physical and cultural characteristics.

archaeology–the study of the life and culture of ancient peoples. Archaeologists dig up the remains of ancient cities and then study the tools, weapons, pottery, and other things they find.

band–a group of people drawn together for a common purpose.

biological diversity–the variety of plant and animal species in a given area.

bond–a force, such as friendship or family ties, that unites people and makes them close.

botanist–a person who studies plants.

botany–the study of plants.

canopy–the top layer of tree growth in a forest.

clan–a social group composed of several families believed to have a common ancestor.

culture–the complete way of living, including ideas, customs, skills, and arts, of a group of people.

deforestation–the clearing of all the trees from a forest.

dialect–the form or variety of a language spoken in a particular region or by a social group.

dysentery–intestinal disease characterized by severe abdominal pain and diarrhea.

ecosystem–a group of plants and animals living together in an environment. An ecosystem also includes all the nonliving things that support them, such as sunlight, water, and minerals.

egalitarianism–the belief that all people should have equal political, social, and economic rights.

elder–an older person with authority and dignity within a community.

evolved–changed gradually over time.

fallow–left unplanted for one or more seasons.

foraging–searching for food.

fossils–hardened remains or traces of plants or animals that lived long ago.

game–wild animals hunted for food or sport.

global village–the modern world, in which people from all over the earth communicate, share experiences, and depend on one another for resources.

habitat–the place where a plant or animal naturally lives and grows.

hunter-gatherers–people who survive by hunting animals and gathering plants for food.

indigenous–people who belong to, or have traditionally lived in, an area; also called native, original, aboriginal, or first people.

initiation ceremonies–the special occasion during which a person becomes a member of a particular society.

leprosy–an infectious disease that attacks the skin, flesh, and nerves.

malaria–a disease of the red blood cells that is caused by parasites and is characterized by severe fever and chills; it is transmitted to people by mosquitoes.

market economy–the system in which people work for wages and use money to purchase goods, food, and services.

menstruation–the periodic discharge of blood and tissue from the uterus.

nutrients–things that help animals and plants live and grow; proteins, minerals, and vitamins are some nutrients.

oral tradition–the handing down of legends and information through the spoken word over many generations.

parasites–plants or animals that live in or on another species called a host; usually parasites harm their hosts by causing disease.

rites of passage–ceremonies that mark a person's going from one stage of life to the next.

ritual–a ceremony, rite, or religious observance.

savanna–a tropical grassland with scattered trees.

seminomad–a member of a group of people who move their homes and belongings several times a year.

slash-and-burn agriculture–farming method by which trees are cut and burned to create a garden patch. Burning releases nutrients into the soil that are used by the planted crops.

sorghum–tropical grass that produces small seeds; grown for grain, syrup, and cattle food.

succession–the regular, orderly pattern of change and growth that an ecosystem goes through over time, ending in a final "climax" community, such as an old-growth forest.

symbiotic–close relationship between two different groups that benefits both.

taboo–anything that is forbidden by tradition.

Third World–the "developing" countries of the world, where most of the people do not have modern consumer goods such as appliances, cars, and televisions; most of the people in the Third World countries are poor and have inadequate water, food, and housing.

totem–an animal, plant, or other natural object taken as a symbol for a family group.

traditional–a way of doing things that has been handed down from generation to generation.

tribe–a group of families and clans who claim a common ancestor.

tropical–describing the region on the earth closest to the equator.

tuber–the short, thick, fleshy part of an underground stem; a potato is one example of a tuber.

INDEX

aetasi, 33
Aka, the, 14
anthropologists, 14, 17, 18, 40
archeological evidence, 18

Bambuti, the, 14
basenji, 32
biological diversity, 14

communication, 58

"Dancers of God," 16
deforestation, 61
dialect, 14
duikers, 14, 32, 34

ecosystem, 20, 23
Efe, the, 6, 8, 14, 18–21, 63, 64
    beliefs of, 50
    belongings and, 27
    children of, 24, 26, 29, 30
    clothing of, 27
    death and, 57
    diet of, 36
    diseases of, 57
    elders of, 24, 29, 52-55
    families of, 27
    height of, 19
    honey gathering by, 34-36
    hunting by, 32-34
    language of, 23, 60
    legends of, 11, 12, 22, 23, 38, 39, 49, 56
    Lese and, 17, 18, 39–47, 51, 52, 62, 63
    marriage among, 31
    men, roles of, 30, 31
    rituals of, 33, 50-55
    society of, 28
    songs and music of, 55
    values of, 27
    women, roles of, 30, 31
egalitarian society, 28
evolution, 20

fossils, 18

global village, 6, 58

hunting and gathering, 8, 15, 17

Iliad, 16
ima, 51, 52
indigenous people, 14, 20
iswa, 36
Ituri River, 13
Ituri Forest, 6, 8, 13, 14, 20, 40, 60, 61

Lese, the, 17, 18, 39–47, 51, 52, 62, 63

Mbuti, the, 14
mota, 33

natural resources, 59
Nile River, 15

Okapi Wildlife Reserve, 7
oral tradition, 23

pharaohs, 15, 16
plantations, 20, 61-63
poison arrows, 16
pygme, 16
Pygmies, 6, 8, 14, 15-19
    art and literature, in, 16
    height of, 18

rain forest, 9, 13, 15, 18, 23
    canopy, 35
    farming in, 40-46
rites of passage, 50-52

savanna, 14
Schweinfurth, Georg, 17
seminomadic peoples, 28
slash-and-burn agriculture, 41-46
Sua, the, 14
symbiotic relationship, 18

taboo, 50
Third World, the, 59
totem, 49
Turnbull, Colin, 17

Zaire, 8, 13, 32, 60, 61

ABOUT THE AUTHOR

Alexandra Siy's interest in the natural world began during the first celebration of Earth Day, when she was ten years old. She studied biology in college and went on to do research in a biotechnology laboratory. Later she earned a master's degree in science education and taught high-school biology and physiology.

Ms. Siy, who lives in Albany, New York, now divides her time between writing and raising her two young children. **Global Villages** continues the theme of the interconnectedness of people and the environment, which she began in the **Circle of Life**, her first group of books for Dillon Press.